CW00555596

OPERATION XX
AND ME
DID I HAVE A CHOICE?

OPERATION XX AND ME

DID I HAVE A CHOICE?

GLYNDWR PHILLIPS

BROWN
DOG
BOOKS

First published 2019

Copyright © Glyndwr Phillips 2019

The right of Glyndwr Phillips to be identified as the author of this
work has been asserted in accordance with the Copyright, Designs
& Patents Act 1988.

All rights reserved. No part of this book may be reproduced, stored
in a retrieval system, or transmitted in any form or by any means,
electronic, electrostatic, magnetic tape, mechanical, photocopying,
recording or otherwise, without the written permission of the
copyright holder.

Published under licence by Brown Dog Books and
The Self-Publishing Partnership, 7 Green Park Station,
Bath BA1 1JB

www.selfpublishingpartnership.co.uk

ISBN printed book: 978-1-83952-014-3
ISBN e-book: 978-1-83952-015-0

Cover design by Andrew Prescott
Internal design by Andrew Easton

This book is printed on FSC certified paper

Printed and bound by CPI Group (UK) Ltd, Croydon CR0 4YY

OPERATION XX AND ME

"The Headmaster wants to see you" strikes fear at any time, but where this would lead I had no idea.

I attended Green Park College in Bath and our swimming lessons were held in the Roman Baths. It was Tuesday morning and as I was walking back to school after the swim I was told to report to the Headmaster. I thought it was someone having a joke, so after break I went to my next lesson, where the teacher asked, "Have you been to the Headmaster's room?" "No Miss," I replied, thinking what would he want with me?

"You'd better go now," I was told.

I tapped on his door, hoping he was not there.

"Come in. There you are. I want you to meet the Captain here. He would like to talk to you," said the Head.

"I am looking for young men with certain talents, real skill with horses and a photographic memory; your Headmaster tells me you have these," the Captain says.

An hour later, to my astonishment, he seems to know more about my past than me. To listen to him I came from another world. Then I realised he was talking about talents and not spelling and writing.

I still did not know why he picked on me.

"I see you are puzzled. It is because of an essay you wrote," he told me and then said, "I am arranging for you to have extra lessons at a gym two afternoons a week." He told me where it was and added that he would meet me there at two o'clock the next day.

The gym was about a mile from the school. A lot of private schools used it but you had to pay extra on the fees. The Captain met me outside right on two o'clock. We went in and I was introduced to a retired Naval Commander who ran it. Then I was introduced to two other lads, one from Bristol and one from Exmouth; they seemed a lot older than me.

"You are here to learn the art of self-defence," we were told, and that we should put ourselves in the hands of the Commander. It had been arranged that we should attend the gym on two afternoons a week.

The Captain then left, saying he would see me in two weeks, back at school.

After we finished at the gym, I thought I would catch an early bus home.

Sometimes, going home to Box, my two friends and I would get off a few stops early and walk the stream, but today by myself I had time to go to the stables before doing my bread round.

At this time I had two jobs. One was exercising the horses, the other was the bread round. This meant riding a bicycle with one big and one small basket full of bread. I had about twelve customers. It was a good five miles journey round for six days a week and I was paid six shillings and sixpence. When I went to school in the village I did the round in the morning but when I went to college in Bath, I had to do it after school, when I got home.

I arrived at the stables the same time as Mr Peter. He had been out with six riders, two on leading reins. I helped him water the horses and rub them down.

"What was I doing home?" he asked me. I told him a little and then he said, "That must be the same person that's been asking about you and your riding."

That night I thought a little about the day, but was soon asleep. When I woke in the morning I remembered we were asked, about six weeks ago, to write what we would like to do when we left school. Well, I wrote things like being a top-class rider, able to speak three different languages and bringing back news from the war: was that the essay the Captain mentioned, I wondered.

School at Pengam 1935-6

I was born in Gelligaer near Bargoed and Mountain Ash in Mid Glamorgan and went to school at Pengam. I had four brothers and three sisters all older than me.

In the cottage garden at Middle Hill with my older brothers and dad in the back

The only work in South Wales was mining so very soon my brothers began to leave and find work in England. Three of them went to work in Northampton in the shoe factories. My eldest brother and a friend set off on their bikes and found jobs in the stone quarries between Box and Corsham. Eventually he found us a cottage in a small village called Middlehill. It was an old coach house, at one time, with a big garden and a high wall all the way round. There were twelve pear and two plum trees. At the bottom was a door that opened on to a wood that at one time had been an orchard. There was a stream and another door leading on to the common.

Playing on the farm

I had two friends. One was older than me, the other about my age and his father owned a big farm. We would play shops in his barn and my friend's mother would give us real chocolate bars to sell in our shop.

When the farmer was cutting the corn, we were allowed very

close to the machine to keep the rabbits in the middle of the field. Then when the last bit was to be cut all the men and the farmer would stand by with their guns to shoot the rabbits as they came out of the corn – sometimes as many as sixty in a field.

Then my brothers began to come home, as there was a lot more work in the area, but this meant they had to sleep in a big tent out on the common as there was not the room in the house. The lady from the big house, who rented us the cottage, lent us the tent and it was big enough for three beds.

About a year or so later we were offered a council house with four bedrooms; this would allow my brothers to sleep in the house. It was on the outskirts of Box, high above the village, called Barn Piece, half way up Quarry Hill. From it you looked out on fields and a big wood. In the woods were old quarries, caves and tunnels.

Moving from the cottage was not easy, to get to Box we had to go under the railway bridge. We called it the Dirty Arch. There was a footpath eighteen inches high and the cows used it to get from one field to another. If it rained it flooded. When the lorry came to move us it could not get across the common, so we had to carry all the furniture a hundred yards. Then when we arrived at Barn Piece the lorry could not get up the hill so we had another two hundred yards to carry it all. We had to put up with mud on our shoes for the next three months until the workmen finished the road.

The move was life-changing, not just for my brothers, but my sisters and I now only had half a mile to get to school and could get home for lunch. There was everything a boy could wish for. A brook with lots of fish, moorhens and their nests, and it was deep enough to swim quite a long way if you didn't mind the reeds. You could walk for hours without walking on a road. There were plenty of rabbits, nut trees for nuts and making bows and arrows, big trees for climbing and in the winter when it snowed we were surrounded by fields for sledging.

My favourite place was the woods and caves where you could always find someone with a fire, roasting potatoes or swedes from the farmer's fields. When it rained you could go into the caves. You had to be very careful, if you went in too far all you had to see with was a piece of burning rubber from the local rubber factory. One day we decided to go back in a cave as far as possible. After about half an hour all the rubber burnt out and we were in there for a good four hours till some of the parents came in after us, with torches.

Soon after this the war broke out. At first it did not affect us but then my brothers and a brother-in-law went into the army, and then we were overloaded with children from London. The young children in our school had to move out to the chapel to make way for them.

It was about this time I became involved with horses. Mr Peter's riding stable was on a railway siding close to Box tunnel; it had no piped water. So in return for mucking out and carrying two buckets six to ten times a day from the spring at the church, up the hill, across the bridge and down to the siding we were allowed to turn the horses out at the end of the day. Which meant riding them bareback to the fields where they grazed.

After some months we became quite good riders. We were then taken out for our first ride with a saddle. We had been riding so long without one it took some time to get used to, but Mike and I became very good riders. Good enough for some of the local gentry occasionally to ask us to race their horses at meets and point to points.

With saddle and bridle

A fortnight later after gym on Tuesday the Captain came again. "I would like to meet your father," he said. "Shall we say two-thirty p.m. on Sunday?"

Mike and me

On the way to school next day my friend Mike said Mr Peter had to go away for a few days and we were to exercise two of the horses. One was Flash and the other Glide On. Knowing these two were retired race horses I had my doubts, but I thought we were good enough riders. So after school we saddled up and away we went. It was alright until we came to Kingsdown Golf course. As soon as Glide On touched the grass we were away. There was no stopping them, not even when we came to the road – straight across we went, and on again. Good job there was no traffic. When we managed to stop them, we stuck to the roads until we came to the Hostel at Hawthorn where all the buses unload. Flash took one look and went mad – he went up, down, up, down and around till he fell on his side. I will never forget it, but I knew if I got off, I would never get on again. We did not tell Mr Peter for some time. He had a saying, "You can always get a good lad but you can't always get a good horse."

On Sunday the Captain turned up and was shown into the front room. In those days most people had a front room for Sundays and important visitors. He was with my father for about an hour and, as he was leaving, he said, "I'll see you in another two weeks."

He had told my father he was looking for a particular boy. "We have picked out twenty from the country, of which only three will be chosen, but we need only one, the others will be backup. Their size is very important, also they have to be good with horses and have a photographic memory. Unfortunately it cannot be a man because of the size. We need your permission for your son to join our team of twenty."

My father was afraid of nothing and no one. One of his friends told me when they were working at the station, loading and unloading ammunition. One night they saw flashing lights round the trucks. No one would go and look. All the men said that 'if they were going to blow up the train, they could do it!' Not your old man! He went out to check on his own but he found nothing.

My mother knew nothing about what was going on. My father told me not to tell her, at the moment, as she would only worry as my brothers and my sister's husband were in the army.

My mum was very strict and worked very hard. With all the ammunition dumps and underground factories we had to take in lodgers. Most of the time there were ten of us to feed and care for.

The invasion was well into France and driving the Germans back and Yanks were everywhere.

The gang in the Box quarries

I was thinking about what sort of work I could do when I left school and had just started shaving about once a month. Around this time girls began to come into my life. The boys and girls would spend hours playing on the tumps and in the woods. When it got dark, we would split up and go different ways, some with girlfriends. On occasion you would have to wrestle for the girl, sometimes as many as two or three different boys – there were always more boys than girls.

A favourite game was 'whip tin', where one person would kick away the tin and the others would run into the woods or hide behind the tumps, then try and get back to kick the tin away without being seen. But if you had your favourite girl it would be some time before you got back.

I was now being put through my paces at the gym. The Commander had me crawl into a concrete pipe fifteen feet by eighteen inches. My job was to pull myself through then work my way back. At first it seemed impossible, but the Commander kept me at it. Once I managed to pull myself backward a few times I got the hang of it and could do it in about thirty seconds, but my toes were quite sore. I was beginning to think that the Commander did not like me. I was working very hard, then he said, "You must come four afternoons a week. I've had a word with your school and it's alright."

I had never liked school – it all seemed like a waste of time… Arithmetic came very easy to me but spelling, reading and writing I gave up on. My parents got very worried about my education and decided to take me away from the village school and send me to a private school in Bath, with two other lads from the village. The name of the school was Green Park College. The first day all the class had a good laugh; to them we were country bumpkins.

At break time some of the bigger lads started to take the 'Mickey' so I picked on the biggest one and got stuck in. They never took the 'Mickey' again. I felt sorry for the lad after, as he turned out to be one of the best. I learned to swim, some French and Algebra, but my spelling did not improve.

At Flapping meeting

We were off to a flapping meeting on Saturday. I was to ride Robin because my weight was six stone, a stone lighter than Mike. I finished third. At the end of the day Mr Peter entered all three ponies in the last race. Off we went, pushing and shoving each other out of the way. I was pushed over by my friend, upside down I went, only to be picked up by the Captain – out of the blue.

"I need to see your father again," he said. "Shall we say two-thirty tomorrow, like before?"

On the Sunday the Captain arrived. "We would like your son to come to London for two days to meet someone and talk about how he would feel if he was chosen for a job with the Intelligence Corps. We are building up a force of about twenty young people. At hand there are only three lads small enough for this assignment. I cannot tell you any more than that your lad is one of them. He is the youngest so he will only be the backup. If you agree, we can arrange something to tell his friends and your lodgers. Do not tell anyone. I will be in touch."

I did not have to wait long.

We travelled up to London by train and took a taxi to a big set of offices. We entered and a policeman asked for some identification. The Captain took something out of his pocket and then we had a badge pinned to our coats. We were shown to a door and down some steps; to me they seemed to go on forever. We came to a door with a soldier who opened it, and in we went. It was like being inside a telephone exchange. We sat down with two other lads who were looking as worried as I felt.

The Captain spoke to them, then after ten minutes an officer came, spoke to the Captain then took us to another room where there were three more officers, rows of chairs, a big screen, film projector and one person in civilian clothes.

"Take a seat, I want to show you some pictures," one of the officers said. Then we were shown a sort of news reel. What part of the world it was, I did not know. There were a lot of fields, trees and a big house with a high wall. Round the top of the wall there was about three feet of barbed wire. To the left of the house another sort of building that looked like a stable block with some good-looking horses.

After the film we were told there were some very important people in the house.

"With the way the war is going we have to get them out, as the nearer our armies get the greater the danger to them. We think they may be shot.

"Now we need one person to help us get some information to them and bring out a photographic picture in his head.

"Only one person is allowed near the wall, he is one of the stable lads. Each day he takes two or three horses in through the gate in the wall, it is not always the same lad, but he has to wait there until the officers come back from their ride. There is time to have a good look around and memorise the layout in the courtyard and where any sentries might be.

"Between the high wall and the stable block is an eighteen-inch concrete pipe which is open on the stable side but has bars on the other end. We can get messages in and out but it is not possible to use a camera. So whoever we send must have three things going for him: he must speak French and a few words of German, have a photographic memory and be small enough to go up the pipe and get out again.

"At ten a.m. the prisoners start their exercise. One of them stands near the end of the pipe. Our job is to get a message to him. We'll tell him to expect a special force dropping in on them and, because the Germans might panic, we need to know where all the prisoners sleep and any information about the positions of any guards and the main force.

"That's it at the moment, except how you get there. A light plane will fly you in. I will now take any questions."

"Well, there is one," I asked. "How do we get back?

It went very silent and then the Captain spoke for the first time. "In all probability the same way, by plane."

Then we were soon on the train on our way home back to the routine of school, training, horses and friends again.

Like any other village, we had our gangs. When we were younger if we were playing cricket one boy would own the bat and wickets so he would bat first, then his mother would call so he would take his bat with him and we would have to wait for him to finish his tea. Football was no better, only one boy had a ball and if he did not want to play or he was on the losing side that would mean – no football.

The hanging tree

Our village was split in two by the Bath road, which ran close to the Box tunnel. We had the hill and woods and the lower part had the field, rivers and brooks. Battles were arranged but after some hard fighting we would all sit down around a fire and divide parts of the woods and field, then peace would be declared for a while.

In the quarries

On a Saturday morning we could walk to Corsham for a matinee at the cinema, we saw films like Old Mother Riley, Laurel and Hardy and lots of cowboys. I think the cowboy films had something to do with an incident, when one of the gang fights was on, they thought they had to hang someone. After some game one lad was picked out. A tree was found, a rope put over and after a big struggle the other end tied round his waist as he was struggling too much to get it round his neck.

He was hauled up for about ten minutes before he was let down. This became the initiation test to join the gang.

On Sundays a lot of Yanks began to ride. Sometimes we would have as many as seventeen horses out every hour. You can imagine the number of buckets we had to carry from the church for the horses to have a drink.

The week after going to London, Mike and I decided to go and look at two horses in a small field in the wood. We then decided we would have a ride round the paddock bareback and without a bridle. We were playing cowboys and Indians when my friend gave my horse a touch on the hindquarters. The horse suddenly shot away and I shot off and bumped my head. At the time I look no notice.

"Are you alright?" asked Mike.

"Just a bit of a headache," I replied.

Well, that night we had the doctor up and he said I'd had a fit and to stay in the house for a while and off the horses. The next day he was back with the Captain. I found out the village doctor also did work for the Army Medical Board at Bristol and had been "put in the picture".

The Captain said, "This will fit in with our plans. We will tell the school and the lodgers you have to be off school for two months. I will send someone to improve your French and give you a few words of German. We will say he is a teacher, to stop your mother worrying."

Six days later the Captain turned up on Sunday unexpectedly. My dad had been to work till about twelve o'clock then all the men would go to the pub; this meant he would not arrive home until two p.m. Mum would have a go at him for drinking and wasting money.

The Captain was given a cup of tea and asked to wait in the

front room till Dad had finished his dinner. By then he would have sobered up.

"It's all set for tomorrow. We travel to London," the Captain told us. "It won't be you going because of your age, you are only backup."

"Number one has broken his arm," we were told when we arrived in London.

"You are still standby," the officer said, then asked me to sign a form. On it they had my age as sixteen next birthday instead of fourteen, someone had made a mistake. I was feeling good knowing I was not going, so I said nothing.

A door opened and another officer said, "Could you come this way, please," and I went into the next office. The Captain spoke with the officer and then turned to me, "It looks like you may have to go as number two has gone down with flu, or something."

I suddenly went all cold.

"We will run through it all again to make sure you have got everything right," the Captain said.

We were driven out to an open space which looked like a field with some underground bunkers. We went into an office and I was given a glass of water and two pills.

The Captain was called away and after some time he came back and said we were to go back to London. On the way he never spoke. I thought all sorts of things, but by now the pills I had taken began to work so things did not seem so bad. By the time we got to the underground offices I felt quite cool.

We were told that the Germans had released all the prisoners and pulled out. So I could go home.

As the Captain put me on the train he said, "We will be in

touch."

Well it was five years before we did, but that is another story.

Time came to leave school; something I had been waiting for, it could not come quickly enough for me. At the time no one thinks that one day you'd wish you were back at school.

My first job was in a garage at Bath. I had to be there at 8a.m. and that meant 8a.m., not five past. For me that meant leaving home at seven and cycling seven miles to work then seven miles home after work. Bikes and cycling become part of life. Well, the job at the garage was not for me, or any other job at the time.

I drifted from one job to another, not knowing what I really wanted, but my mother would not let me finish a job before I had another. If you wanted work you could soon find it. I worked in those days for the money and spent it as quick. I could write a hundred pages on my first two years but I will stick to those I remember most, like when the fair came to the village for the first time after the war.

I got to know one of the lads that worked with the fair. I would help him with his work then at night, when the fair was busy, I would ride all night for nothing. In those days the music came from in a big book form, you took one out and replaced it with another. My job was to change the music over, which meant jumping on and off with the thing going round. I soon became quite expert and the envy of all the village kids. The boss of the fair offered me a job to travel with them, but my mother said no.

My two friends at the stable and myself wrote to one or two racing stables but as usual my mother said no, so off my two friends went, leaving me behind. I now began to understand my father and his drinking. Every job I got was no better than the last one and, as my father went through life doing a job with no future, I was heading the same way. I found my answer in smoking and drinking. As I looked older than my age, I had no trouble getting served.

One job I liked was working on a lorry as driver's mate, hauling wheat from the station to the flour mill. Each bag weighed 2 1/4 cwts. Sometimes we would have to deliver coal, which meant carrying the sack on your back for twenty to fifty yards all day. My father thought at fifteen years it was too much. So ended my job on the lorry.

My next job was back with horses. I went in to a gentleman's service looking after three hunters. The man of the house was a gentleman but his wife was no lady. I was not allowed to whistle and I had to always wear a hat when exercising the horses. This made people tip their hat and say, 'Good Morning'. In those days country people would not look to see who you were. I had a laugh or two – if only they knew who they had tipped their hats to.

One of the hunters

One of my jobs was to take the three horses to the meets. When Sir and his party arrived, by car, they went off hunting and I sat in the car, sometimes for four or five hours. When they returned they went home in the car, leaving me to ride back with the horses. I loved the riding part of the job and looking after the horses but cleaning shoes and coats etc. every morning, I got a bit fed up. The good side was one of the horses had to be exercised three or four hours a day. This meant I could get right away from the place and go where I liked.

One day I was turning the other two horses out into a field a mile away. We had got to know each other well so, to save carrying the bridles back from the field, I would just use a rope halter. I had just got outside the gate when something moved in the hedge, and the two horses just took off. I had no way of stopping them. They went across one road junction out on to the main road, up the left-hand side until they were opposite the field gate again. They then went straight across the road and stopped at the gate. I don't know who was most scared, me or the horses. It was the first time on that road and I had not passed a car or a lorry.

This job did not last long. I liked it but the money was only fifteen shillings a week and I did not see eye to eye with the lady of the house. She wanted me to clean out her chickens. I said, "Sorry but it's not my job." Next day the old gentleman asked me to keep her ladyship happy and she would give me some eggs once in a blue moon. So I said I would clean out her chickens once in a blue moon. She did not ask me again.

My Father worked for a civil engineering firm so he got me a job as a tea boy and looking after the traffic lights. I did not think I would give twenty-five years to this firm! I left four or five times but never stayed away for more than six months at a time. It was my first meeting with Bert who was foreman, one out of about six who had a big influence on my life. The job was a sewer in the village of Hilperton and at that time most of the work was done by hand. We had one old digger, one water pump and a lorry – that was that.

After the lorry had dropped us off, it then set out to pick up about twenty German prisoners. As the war was now over each firm was allowed so many prisoners a day. At first it was very difficult, but they were glad the war was over too. Well they now met Bert and I think they wished they were back on the front line. They called him "Lomas", a name he would carry to his grave.

The Germans were good workers and we would bring coffee in for them and swap it for their tea ration. In those days cigarettes were hard to get so one of my jobs was to produce about three hundred a day for forty to fifty men. This meant a trip in the morning and again after dinner as each shop would only let each customer have twenty. It was a good mile into town and then I had to walk from shop to shop to produce the three hundred needed.

Bert was a hard man. Two or three times a month men with bars or a pick axe would go up behind him, but someone would always shout out. I don't think they shouted for Bert's sake, because now I began to wish him dead. Every day he would never give up, he would give everybody four or five jobs at a time then ten minutes later, if he saw you look up, he would ask if you were looking for another job.

Well, I could go on forever about this man but as I really got to know him I thought he should have got an OBE or something.

He gave everything he had to give to his job, he never treated any one man better than another, no matter what he was or what he had done. One day a man put a pick through his foot. "Damn me, Dominic, a new pair of wellingtons this morning," was all he said.

I decided to go back with horses. I was offered a job in a riding school at Larkhall in Bath. Most of the customers were between four and fourteen years old. One day I had two four-year-olds on leading reins going up this big hill, about one in ten. A lorry loaded with hay came by us and I could see he was never going to make it. Suddenly it started to run back down the hill. Thank goodness the driver turned the lorry into the bank but as it hit the bank it turned over in the middle of the road. I got the two little girls back to the stable only to find they had both wet themselves.

This job meant a lot of walking. I had horses in fields miles away and when the snow came, I had to carry hay on my back out to them. The boss also had a goat and one of my jobs was to feed it; this meant a round trip of four miles a day. One day I got all the work up together so I could finish early. Off I went on my bike back to Box to help my mate finish up his horses so we could go to the pictures. I was leaning on the hay fork and suddenly I could not move, my legs seemed paralysed. My friend managed to get me on my bike and get me home, where my mother put me to bed. I still don't know what it was but after ten days it went as quick as it came. I never went back to that job.

So off I went to try my hand at fitting. As I was waiting for the fitter along came the foreman carpenter and said, "Come with me." I said, "No, I was waiting for the fitter."

"I've seen your dad, and he said to take you under my wing," he told me. So there went my ambition to be a fitter.

Well, I was put with a chap who came out of the forces on a B Scheme. You got out first if you had a trade. He was a very nice person whose father had a builder's business in the village of Box, so he was just waiting his time. After buying carpentry tools I jacked it in as my heart was not in it.

At that time I was a corporal in the Army Cadet Force. The officer, who ran the force in the village, told me he was going to start a riding school and asked if I would help him run it. So I'm back with the horses. Well, it was not an easy job getting a riding school going from scratch, as Mr Mac was soon to find out. He knew nothing about horses, his daughter had a pony and she was a good rider.

Well, Mr Mac was a good business man and, as we were surrounded with RAF camps, he managed to talk two officers in the camps into allowing the WRAF to take riding lessons as part of their sports days, twice weekly.

So four afternoons a week we would take six horses to the camps and teach young ladies who had never been near a horse before. In the end it turned out to be a bit of fun.

After about nine months Mr Mac was losing money so he sold up all the horses and I was looking for a job again.

At this time one of my brothers was working for a plant firm and got me a job on a calf dozer. It was quite different from all my other jobs. They would drop you off miles away from anywhere and say, "Ring when you're finished and we will pick you up." The job was to fill in all the trenches, sometimes as much as four miles long, on farmland. Most of the farmers would get a government grant to lay water pipes in all their fields.

I was now sixteen and once the low loader dropped you off without any transport you then had to find lodgings. You can imagine what sort of places one had to put up with, some good, some bad and some beyond imagination. So the first time I got back home, after a week away, I saw a motor bike for sale at Bath. I had never been on a motorbike before but, full of confidence I bought it – an old 'one fifty' which you had to pump oil into the engine every one or two miles. It was not easy trying to work everything at once, for the first time, through a city like Bath but we got back in one piece. On Monday the job I'd been given was about six miles away, so I thought 'no lodgings this time'. After about two miles on the bike I found myself upside down in the road, the bike as well. I was lucky so I got on again, but I learned one thing. I was not as good as the chaps on the speedway.

I seemed to be able to get more out of a machine than most people so three days' work would be done in one and a half, and the boss would ask, "Have you missed two or three fields?" I was then given one or two more interesting jobs.

The village of Box had just started a football team. I loved kicking a ball about but never played in a league. After a trial or two I managed to get in to the team and football became my first love. I was fortunate to be playing with some good men who, had it not been for the war, might have been professionals by now. I would play Saturdays in the league and Sunday mornings we would have a kick around. There could be as many as thirty lads turn up so we would play fifteen-a-side. Then in the afternoon I'd get on my bike and ride to Corsham and play in their youth team.

I played on the right wing or centre forward and scored quite a lot of goals. In a village like Box you were a hero through the week and Cup Final days were out of this world, but without the other players you would be nothing.

The gang

We had our Youth Clubs and we used them as meeting places, not for games or pleasure. It would all start out innocent enough until gangs from other villages and towns came and hung about outside. The trouble would start when they were let in. On one occasion things were going along very nicely then, for no reason, it all began to go wrong and billiard balls started to fly across the hall and chairs came through the air. It was a miracle no one was badly hurt. The youth leader, who was in her fifties and had worked so hard, came through the door: all the lads and girls did not know what to say. This poor lady had gone against the community for a mixed club and now the hall was a mess.

On another occasion most of our girl friends were rehearsing for the Christmas show in the chapel. In those days the lights were all gas and we thought we would frighten the girls when they came downstairs, so we turned them off. We waited for a while and then decided to go for a walk. We went further than we intended and when we got back there were people everywhere. The gas lights had gone out but the gas was still on and some of the young people were quite ill. We were cowards, we did not tell anyone for a long time.

Fighting went on between gangs but we had some honour. We would not think of using knives or chains. If you did your friends would turn on you. Mind, you were allowed to use stones or shoot with a bow and arrow but you had to be a long way away. We also had a game called 'Done' where you stood on top of a tump with an air rifle loaded with potato. The lads would hide behind other tumps and keep popping their heads up, and the first one hit would change places with the one with the gun.

I think parents are wonderful. My mother would say, "You are not to go out with that boy, he's got a bad name." His mother was probably saying the same about me. I suppose every man had to prove himself but once you got a reputation someone would always try to prove they were better and make it difficult not to do anything about it.

Our main entertainment was the Picture House at Hawthorn

and dances most Saturdays at site one and site fourteen. We had good times at site fourteen till one night things got out of hand. There were all nationalities drinking as if beer was going to stop being made. That night the dance had an extension till twelve o'clock. It never made it to twelve. At nine o'clock the balloon went up, glasses came flying through the air, then bottles. Women started to scream, blood seemed to be everywhere. People made for the cloakrooms but the attendants had left their posts. Everybody started jumping over the counter, coats were everywhere and dozens went home with the wrong one. There was so much damage done the hall never opened again. So that left site one, and it was not long before the same thing happened there, but we had a lot of fun first. A favourite game on the way home was to stop in a field and see who could ride on the back of the cows at night. You can imagine what happened to our clothes.

As we got older the lads started to drift to Bath to the Pavilion or the Drill Hall. We would read in the papers where the trouble was and then tempt providence. The Bath lads did not like us dancing with their girls, or taking them home; after one or two incidents it worked itself out. It was quite easy to get the wrong girl, she could live three miles away. By the time you got to her door the train started blowing its hooter and you had about twenty minutes to get to the station. There was always trouble with the soldiers and airmen, so if you left the girl right away and ran all the way you would just catch it, or you had to walk the six miles home. There was always plenty of company, and by the time you got to Box there could be as many as seven or eight of us. This was how I made friends with a lad from Belgium, whose mother had married a chap from the village. He was the only grandson of a well-known garage set-up that dealt with Mercedes, and his grandfather would send him an allowance every month. He was only sixteen and we were not old enough to drink but he drank gin like water. It soon became our favourite drink. I don't think it did us any good.

Back at the village it was all happening. They had started dances at the Bingham Hall and with the Hostel not far away we got a lot of Irish men coming in, after the pubs closed, and they didn't want to pay. There was one lad in the village built like 'Garth' and he would pick them up and give them a shake till their money dropped out of their pockets. He would pick up a shilling for the dance and put the rest back in their pockets, saying, "In you go, Paddy, and be a good chap."

I was eighteen and away again in lodgings, this time in a place called Teffont with one pub, a stream and a lot of hills. The landlady was a fragile woman, as she passed your tea half of it ended in the saucer. Later I found she suffered from Parkinson's disease. Her husband was a big man but quite a laugh in the pub. When he went to the toilet, he would take his glass of cider with him and when he came back it was only half full, so you would buy him another pint. After a week I got a bit suspicious and discovered he was filling up a big jar in his garden for the weekend. He was a dry old character and when a chap had just fallen from the church spire, he said, "It's not the falling they mind, it's the sudden stop at the bottom they don't like." They had two nice daughters, one was ten years older than me and would make up any tale to visit the fields where I was working.

The job seemed to be going well when out of the blue a gentleman was stood by my side.

"Good morning," he said. I thought, what have I done now? "You know this is Government property and the work done here is top secret?" he said.

"Not really. I can see there must be an army post or something behind the high fence," I replied.

He then looked me straight in the eye. "You don't remember me, do you? Does Operation Twenty mean anything to you?"

I went very cold, "No, sir. I must get on with my work now, sir."

He put his hand in his pocket and produced a card with his identification and a photo of me when I was about fourteen.

I just froze. When I managed to speak again, I said, "I think I remember you now sir, you were the civilian gentleman in London four or five years ago."

Then he said, "This job you are doing here is no coincidence, it took a lot of engineering. I think you are coming up for a medical for the army soon. Do this little job and you could fail that medical, or do you want to do two years in the army?"

Well, six months earlier I had volunteered but was told to go home and wait seven months. I now felt differently. "Have I got a choice?" I asked.

"Now it's not like that," he said, then told me what he would like me to do. "There is a chap in a grey A60 parked down the road. He's been hanging about for three weeks. He uses the pub in the village. We think he is on to us, so you are our backup."

"You could have told me weeks ago," I said.

"Yes, but we did not think we would need you for sure," he replied.

"So what do you want me to do?" I asked.

"We think someone inside is giving him information, we want to know who. By the way, that is not just an army camp, so when you get near that fence catch your blade in it then you will have to go in to the camp to report it. It could be a talking point in the pub tonight."

Unfortunately one of the wires on the fence got caught on the track of my machine and made a bigger hole than I wanted. Then I made my first mistake. I should have gone through the gate and not the hole to report it. I then knew what he'd meant when he said it was not just an army camp. I was put in a Land Rover and taken to the guard room. After answering a lot of questions I was able to convince them I was not lying, so they let me go.

Well, that night I kept a close watch on the chap with the A60 and, when he got out of the car, I followed him into the pub.

Half an hour later a man with a beard came in and started talking to him. He then took a cigar out of his pocket and gave that to him. The chap with the cigar then went to the toilet but when he came back the cigar was quite a bit thinner. That must be a different cigar, I thought, so I drank up and left.

Parked a little way along the road was a black Rover. I walked up to it and tapped on the window, the back door opened and I got in. I told the civilian gentleman what I saw and just as I was getting out of the car a voice from the front asked, "How did you know we were in this car?"

"I've been watching you from the pub for the last two hours," I told him. As he turned round, I could see his face – it was the Captain who had got me involved four years ago."

"Good night," he said, "I think we will make a professional out of you yet."

Next day, about ten o'clock, my machine broke down and I went back to the village to phone up for a fitter. On the way back the Rover pulled up beside me. "Can I give you a lift?" the Captain said. As I got in, he added, "Oh, and by the way, there was no need to make such a big hole in the fence – one big enough for a man to crawl through would have done the job. We managed to catch both men red-handed thanks to you." He then put twenty pounds in my hand, saying, "Mum's the word. We will be in touch," and drove off.

An hour later the fitter turned up and took one of the clutches out. "This is a job for the workshop," he said. So I went home with him. It took two days to get the spares then we went back to get the dozer going again. The fence had been repaired, I finished the back filling then returned to the yard.

My next job was a reservoir, and it was a big one with a pipeline, too. I got lodgings in a house about two miles away with a lady called Mrs Small. She was the biggest woman I have ever seen. There were three lads staying there, they worked for the Forestry Management. I did not stay long; it was cold water to wash in the morning and get your own dinner out of the oven at night. I managed to get in the local pub with another plant driver. My night life was just about to begin.

My first dance away from home no one knew who I was, a new face at a village hop. I think I must have enjoyed myself. I was minus a tie next day – one I had saved up for, it was white silk with ladies in swimsuits on it and had been the envy of all my mates. They told me I had given it away to a lad who could not take his eyes off it.

I was driving the tractor and trailer with a load of iron pipes down through the fields, which were about one in ten. Suddenly the back wheels lifted off the ground, with only brakes on the back wheels. I found myself picking up speed. What happens is the trailer with only two wheels on goes faster than the tractor: the weight on the trailer pushes the tractor faster and faster. When you touch the brakes the back of the tractor lifts off the ground so the only thing to do is turn into the bank, or whatever is there. I think the Lord above was with me as the next two gates were open. I was now travelling at twice the speed the tractor was made for. I got through one gate and took one post with me from the other. When I told my friend he just laughed. "That can happen to anyone," he said. "It happened to me just last week, but I was going into town and the whole lot tipped over – tractor, trailer and the pipes."

I was soon back in the yard with nothing for my machine to do so I was sent out with one of the gangs to a well-known Agricultural College. A couple of the lads decided to go out on the river one lunch time, so we got into a flat boat with a long rope on it tied to the bank. After going up the river and across it for about a hundred yards one of the lads said, "Right, put your sombreros on. I don't want you getting sunstroke while I tell you a story – 'How we did it in the desert'." He then grabbed the rope and started to pull us into the bank. As he did so, he winked at me. I guessed what he was going to do, but the other lad was not slow. As we got near the bank, he did what we were going to do, only a second before we did. The boat stopped when he pushed against it to jump clear of the water and on to the bank. My friend and I jumped into the river just as we had planned for him.

The next day we had to put scaffolding under a water tower. This was seventy feet up. We had just finished putting the last plank in place when the one we were standing on moved, about an eighth of an inch. Well, it felt just like a hundred feet. I had my hand on a scaffold pole but my mate did not. We didn't see him for a week and he would not go up under the tank again.

After about three weeks of just cleaning pipes I decided to go back to the old firm who were doing a sewer job at Potterne. It meant working with Bert again and it seemed he had forgotten everybody's name but mine. He would have me cleaning the inside of the mixer, then after five minutes he'd be calling my name again. One day he wanted some pipes up in the village but he'd sent the lorry to Swindon so he had no transport. He said to me, "We'll use the big dumper."

Two of the men loaded nine-inch pipes on till I could not see over the top. I would have to lean out over the side to see where we were going.

"I haven't got a licence to go on the road, and I can't see where we are going," I told Bert.

"I'll stand on the top and tell you where to go," he replied.

"What if we meet a policeman?" I asked.

"Just run the beggar over," was his answer.

Bert would not let anything or anyone get in the way of the job, but we did have some good times, like Christmas. The day before we finished work a lot of the men would go to the pub, and by twelve o'clock some had already had a few pints, so that by the time the lorry should pick us up the driver was well away. Again with no licence I had to drive them to the pub, and that was not the end of it. By three o'clock we still had to get home so I had to sit in the middle of the cab with my feet on the brakes and the clutch and one hand on the steering wheel. Well, we got home alright.

Our job was spread over about a mile, which meant Bert had to ride a bike from one end to the other. One of the lads, Mick, would let the tyres down and Bert could not understand why he kept getting punctures. The funny thing was that he would always pick on Mick to take it to the garage for repair, where Mick would ask the man to pump up the type and charge Bert for a repair.

One day I was digging a trench for a water service when along came Bert: "If you are going to sing and dig, then sing something with a quicker tempo. Let me show you." He then grabbed the spade and started digging like a man gone berserk, then said, "That's the way."

"Anyone can do that for five minutes," I protested. I'd had just about enough and asked for my cards and money to be ready on the Friday.

Bert just smiled and walked away. At the end of the week I asked, "Well, where are my cards?"

"Get in the lorry and don't be so daft," was the reply I got.

Later, I got my own back. I was levelling off the top of the filters when I saw Bert behind the hedge, so I picked up a stone and let fly. Bert came out shouting.

"Sorry Bert," I said, "I thought you were a dog." After that he left me alone for a week or two.

Me with a trencher

One of my brothers, Ivor, worked for Smith & Lacy and drove one of the Alan Parsons trenchers. It had a chain with about twelve buckets going round and round picking up the earth, dropping it onto a conveyor belt and leaving a pile of earth on the side of the trench for back filling. At that time it was a great machine but had seventy-two nipples that had to be greased twice a day and fourteen different levers. To look at it the first time it seemed impossible for one man to drive. Ivor said if I wanted to go back on plant, there was a job going. So I went. Four of us were sent to Oxford, my brother digging the trench, John, who was to be in and out of my life for the next thirty years, and me helping with putting in the pipes.

Trencher

We were there for about six weeks. My brother soon finished the trench and was off to another job. I would travel home at weekends but John would stay. Well, we were all sat down to tea one day when one of the children, who was about six, said, "I saw John kissing mummy, Dad."

I didn't know what to do or where to go, it was very embarrassing, but nothing was said or done. It was a bit more experience for the future – always keeps an eye out for the children.

In the evenings a neighbour would come around, she was about thirty years old and had a nine-year-old boy. I think she was divorced. I started to take her out. She had another boyfriend who was quite a bit older and I think she was using me for her last fling before she got married, but we enjoyed each other's company.

The two sisters 1950

This job came to an end and I was working away at Collingbourne Ducis, only travelling home at the weekends, when I heard on the grapevine that Mr Peter had been kicked by a horse. I went down to the stable to find out how he was but he was in hospital and two young ladies were looking after the horses. On the Monday I packed in my job and went to work for the 'old firm', which meant I could help out with looking after the horses while Mr Peter was in hospital. It seemed fate had struck again. I did not know it then but one of these girls would one day be my wife. The two young ladies were sisters. At first this was a problem, but after a week things began to solve themselves. Another chap, Vivian, who came to the stable, took a liking to the youngest so he would take her home on the back of his motor bike, which left the other to catch the bus or walk. I had quite a good motor bike at that time but was still a learner. We had said very little to each other by then but I took off my L plates and said, "Jump on". We were doing very well, then just as we got in to Corsham there were a lot of people in the road and a police car parked up. A policeman was waving me down, I did not know what to do, then suddenly the bike started to go from under me. I then realised that the big lorry, that was stopped ahead, had left oil over the road. I took a chance and opened up, the bike did the rest. It must have looked quite professional as the policeman put up his hand and waved me on. That was the first time we spoke other than about horses. She asked me in for a coffee and from then on we became good friends.

In the woods 1951

The path to the quarries 1951

Audrey would be waiting for me to get home from work so this meant a quick wash, something to eat, a check on the stables then either a walk through the woods or a cycle ride back to Corsham. Then I'd return to Box by nine p.m. to meet my mates; we were now up to about eight pints of beer a night!

Mr Peter came out of hospital so we were no longer needed at the stables and Audrey got a job at Melksham. This meant me going to Corsham or us meeting half way. We were soon to be married, but for some reason this did not seem to make much difference to my way of life. I still went out to the pub at night and to Bath or Bristol at weekends, not thinking about my wife and what she would like to do. She always seemed to have her head in a book and be quite happy. I look back now and think about what sort of a life she must have had and how she put up with me. We had very little money yet I would spend more on myself than I gave her to look after the house. Well, it wasn't a house, we had just a room rented in someone else's, so when our son was born, we had to find somewhere to live. So I left the firm I was working for and got a job with one that had a contract with the Admiralty, at Copenacre. This seemed to work for the Council as they gave us a wartime bungalow after six weeks. It was on the same site as my wife's parents, so it made life a bit better for her.

OLD ENGLISH BROUGHAM 1876

TO HIRE, CONTACT   BILL PETER··
                                        LOWER ASHLEY STABLES
                                        BOX, WILTS.

I enjoyed working for this new firm. I drove one of the lorries. There were two shafts, one each side of a boundary fence, one inside and one outside. On the inside were Admiralty Police who checked you in and out. I was working from inside the fence, the crane would lift a skip full of stone from the bottom of an eighty-foot shaft then tip it on to the lorry. It took about four skips to a load, then I would drive out of the gate down past the other shaft where a person would look out of the office window, put his hand up to allow you to keep going to the tip. There was a lot of fiddling going on that was not in my nature so I was soon on the move again, back to work once more for the 'old firm'.

This job took me to different places, one week forty miles away, the next two miles. It wasn't very exciting, one minute you were digging a trench and the next a lorry or a roller. In those days we had a lot of things left over from the war. It was nothing to find no brakes on the roller or the steering was no good.

On one occasion we were towing the roller with the lorry as we had a long way to go. Well, it was alright until we came to a hill. The lorry driver was looking in the mirror but I was looking at him from the side and shouting for him to go faster, as the weight of the roller was too much for the brakes. Without the engine going I could not use the gears. One frightened driver suddenly realised what I was saying, just in time, as the tow-rope was just about to touch the back wheel of the lorry. He took his foot off the brake and started to leave the roller behind. By the time we got to the bottom of the hill we were travelling at twenty miles an hour. I must hold the world's speed record for a road roller.

I still played football on Saturdays for Box Rovers. Our main opposition was from Box Hill and Colerne, two teams within three miles of us. Well, you can imagine what the supporters were like. On one occasion a woman came on to the field with her umbrella and hit the centre half because he had fouled the centre forward. We soon got out of that league by winning the cup two years running. We now had to travel a lot further for our football.

In the paper! (me far left)

Box Rovers 1955–56

OPERATION XX and me

PROGRAMME PRICE 1d.	POOLE TOWN FOOTBALL CLUB THE STADIUM · WIMBORNE ROAD Tel. POOLE 790	SATURDAY OCTOBER 12th

WESTERN LEAGUE, Div. II.

POOLE TOWN

Colours—Red & White Shirts, Black Shorts

RIGHT   LEFT

Kirk

Nugent 2   Drummond 3

Vowles 4   Drinkwater 5   Kellard 6

Frame 7   Gorman 8   Hindle 9   Corbett 10   Oosthuizen 11

Referee : Mr. G. A. Bell (Southampton)	Linesmen : Mr. D. Misselbrook Mr. J. R. Cousins

Melrose 11   Ford 10   Phillips 9   Strong 8   Biggs 7

Lyke 6   Ashman 5   Garrett 4

Curtis 3   Rogers 2

Cook

LEFT   RIGHT

CLANDOWN

Next match at the Stadium —
SOUTHERN LEAGUE

POOLE v BEDFORD TOWN

WEDNESDAY, OCTOBER 16th, 1957   Kick-off 3 p.m.

Programme

51

When I was twenty-five the thing I had waited for came too late: a scout had been sent to watch the game. After the match he said I could go to Swindon for a trial. I'd tried two semi-professional clubs before and I knew their players did not want to know you. At first it seemed odd, because I played for the love of the game, not the money, so professional football was not for me.

I played for Box Hill and then back to Box Rovers and was lucky to finish with twelve cups and medals, where better players than me played all their lives and ended up with nothing. I suppose I paid for it by having two operations, one on each knee, which give me great pain still. With my love for the game, I would be out on the field today if possible. I built myself some memories, good and bad, but I would not be without them.

My life began to change. Looking back it sometimes frightened me, as for my world to get better someone else's would get worse. One incident was when a very nice person who drove an Alan Parson's trencher got killed a week after letting me try my hand on it. He'd come off a motor bike. I became first choice to replace him and did not give it a second thought, as it made a big difference to my money. I think I must have dug hundreds of miles of trench with that machine.

The next job was in Trowbridge, excavating a trench for a water main through an old American Army Camp. When they put down a road, they put down a road! We must have pulled out concrete lumps as big as tables, but in the end, we got through it.

In those days no Authority knew where anything was. The Southern Electricity Board representative, with drawing in his hand, said, "Yes, it's a 11,000-volt cable and it's over there." So on we go. Then out comes the farmer and says, "It's right where you're digging!"

I say, "No, I'm told it's over there."

Well, the farmer was right. We hit it. Bang! it went. It was on the wrong side of the road and it was a 22,000-volt cable. The chap in the trench ran for his life. I knew if I touched the ground, I'd be dead. So I jumped out far into the air. The hand of providence had come to my aid once more.

The job was not going well, we had no foreman and an engineer would look in on us now and again. Three weeks later we were sent a man from upcountry. I had worked on a job where he had been in charge of the concreting. I did not like him one bit. It began to snow and the hut where we had our lunch and dinner became further away. Instead of moving the hut with the job, the foreman said we couldn't use it for our ten-minute break, so I left again.

That evening one of the office staff came to the house and said I had left them in a bit of a hole as I was the only plant driver on the firm who could drive the trencher. The firm had been good to me – at one time they had put me through my driving test and had never refused me a job. So I said I would find them a driver, and got my brother to take the job. He got on very well with the foreman. I think someone night have had a word in his ear.

I got work on the bigger plant machines on a job near Bristol with piece workers, laying a telephone duct. I was to take over from another driver who had not done any digging for four weeks. He told me, "It's solid rock and they won't put the digger off hire at the moment because it takes six weeks to get another one. You just turn up each day and then go home at twelve o'clock, but make sure you get your bonus from the chap when he comes round at the end of the week."

Well this went on for another four more weeks. It did not look like the rock was going to go away, so I was put off hire and sent to a job at Woodstock, near Oxford. This was to lay one-inch water pipes round an estate and drop some concrete rings into the middle of some springs about six feet deep. The foreman I had never worked with before, he was a nice person named John Evans but the other chap was a mate of mine called John. My job was to drive us to work, which meant leaving home at six-thirty in the morning, dig trenches all day and drive back home at night, getting back at about ten o'clock. It was a long day.

One place we had to dig a trench was through a wood, up a slope about one in ten with a lake at the bottom. The foreman said, "It looks like a hand job."

"Your brother Ivor would dig it somehow," said John.

So I travel the trencher up through the wood, thinking, 'What have I been talked into?' I'd only got to start slipping on some roots or a track chain break and we'll all end up in the lake. We got to the top alright, and once we dropped the buckets and started digging, I felt a bit better, but all the time I was thinking, 'What would I tell them back at the yard if things went wrong? "Your digger is in the bottom of the lake!"'

Things went well on the digging and laying the pipes, but when it came to dropping the concrete rings down into the springs it was a different matter. We could not get the rings level. So it meant someone had to strip off and with an iron bar move some big stones from under the one side. John volunteered to have a go, with little success. So I stripped off. The water was as cold as ice and we had to find a bit of high ground to stand on and use the iron bar, not knowing what we were trying to move. Well, in the end I had to go down and have a look. We got over the problem by lifting up the rings and I managed to go down and move the stones by hand. Thank goodness the sun was out.

The next day the lorry arrived to move my machine to another job. I saw John a week later and he said the driver they had now to take them to work did not arrive on the job till ten-thirty. He was a strong union man and would only drive at forty miles an hour, and would stop dead at ten o'clock for lunch.

I never seemed happy with this firm so back I went to the 'old firm'. This job was in a village called Biddestone, and landed me with about sixteen Irish men. As the saying goes, 'the money was poor but the craic good'.

It turned out of be one of those jobs where the supervision was poor and nothing went right. I was the only person working for the firm, all the others were subcontractors, so nobody cared what was done right as long as they got a good pay packet at the end of the week.

We had two things that didn't go together – rock and running water. All the work you did in the day would be ruined by people turning the pumps off at night, so all the pipes would be floating and, in those days, it was all Compo joints.

As I said, the craic was good, there was never a dull moment. We had one woman came running up the road, shouting, "There is a dead man in the ditch," but it was only one of the lads had missed the van and walked from Bath, stopping off at a few pubs on the way, and was fast asleep in the ditch.

About three o'clock there was a roar and we all looked up to see Paddy, across the field, running after a woman. He never looked like catching her, then suddenly she went out of sight, and so did Paddy. The woman was one of two who hung around the job in the afternoons. Well, we didn't see Paddy till going home time, one of the lads said, "You've not earned much money today, Paddy."

"I've had a walk in the sun, a drink in six pubs, a good sleep and the love of a good woman, who needs money?" was his reply.

On one afternoon the fitter and his mate came out to the tractor and trailer, it had broken down in the tip. Around this time guns were like playthings and the fitter's mate had got two forty-five colts from somewhere. So they decided to go pheasant shooting on the estate adjoining the tip. The next thing I knew was the fitter's van coming down the road. He stopped and said, "You haven't seen us today," and drove on.

I was soon to find out why. That night the police came knocking on my door. What had happened was the keeper had taken the keys out of the van and rung the police. But keys were no problem to fitters, they just joined the wires together and were away. The police had traced them through the name on the van and interviewed them before coming to me. They knew there was a third person. A police sergeant and an officer said they had been told by the other lads that I was the third person. I lost my temper and told them to get out, or I would put them out. I knew they were lying, as I knew the third person was the tractor driver.

The next day I was walking down the road to fill up one of the pumps and a car pulled up beside me. I felt sick, it was the Captain, now a commander. "Have you got a minute?"

"Is there a choice?" I asked.

"This won't take long, it's about the guns. Where did they come from? Did the Irish lads have anything to do with them?" he questioned.

"No" I replied, "and I was not the third man."

"I'll see you get an apology. We must keep you clean, and thanks for your time. We'll be in touch." He was off again.

The next day the police sergeant turned up, this time full of apologies. At that time one or two guns had been coming to light, the IRA was mentioned and a forty-five colt bullet was found in a dead pheasant. I think the lads were fined fourteen pounds each.

I was asked to take charge of the mixing plant on the next job at Boscombe Down. It was my first look at work from that side of the fence. After we had been running a while, I was told to get everything shipshape. About two days later five or six cars arrived on site, and out stepped some very well-dressed gentlemen. As they disappeared into an office, I was left to face one gentleman with a camera. I had taken all the men off the mixers and plant and told them to keep out of sight, so when the photographer arrived it looked like a dead town. My first big step and I had made a mess of it. Other things on site had gone from bad to worse, so my little mistake never made it into the firm's Once a Year Book.

After all the comings and goings of the bosses, they finally gave up. I did not know the reason, but as you go higher up the ladder you find no one wants to be connected to a bad job. Four weeks later, things began to come round again and the job was back on the right road. Had we been left alone in the first place, things would have been a lot better.

As usual, there were a few comedians. We were blessed with two lads from Liverpool. We never knew what was coming next. About ten o'clock one of the dumpers would be missing and we found out one of the lads had driven to the camp gate then nipped back to see his landlady. The next time the dumper went missing, two of the other lads took some rope and pegs, found the dumper hidden outside the camp and they drove the pegs two feet into the ground then tied the rope round the axle so it could not be seen. About an hour later Bill comes walking back, (he told me he'd been to the shop for cigarettes) started the dumper but couldn't move it. We would still find him missing two or three times a week, but his mate more than made up for his larking about.

When Bill was broke, he would go to the top of the concrete plant and take bets that he'd jump off. He must have jumped off about ten times and only hurt himself once.

Boscombe Down was an experimental place and one of the things at that time was a rocket fixed to the end of each blade of a helicopter. I think it was for lifting loads off the ground. We were set up about a hundred yards from where this was being tested, twenty-four hours a day. They would get it going then fire the rockets; the noise was deafening. The people running the experiment all had ear muffs but we did not, and suffered. As far as I know it was only flown once.

My private life was non-existent at this time. I left home at six-thirty and arrived back at seven-forty-five. I just lived for Saturday's football in the afternoon and the bright lights of Bath or Bristol at night. Like many men, I never gave a thought to the wife. Straight into the bath, on with the suit, pick up my mates and down to the local pub, talk about the football of the day, then on to Bath or Bristol.

We had a set routine: first we would visit six or seven pubs, find out where the life was or where there was likely to be trouble, jump in a taxi and away. If it was to a dance, we would have to get tickets before nine o'clock as the dance hall tickets would be sold out by then. When we'd bought them, we'd go back to the pub till ten-thirty, then on to the bar at the dance hall till eleven-thirty, which left us half an hour for dancing. This sometimes caused a lot of trouble because there were no partners left. I think it was called separating the men from the boys. The women always seemed to go for the man who did not care. This went alright some weeks, but there were a lot of servicemen around the area and always about fifty or sixty in each dance hall, so you can imagine what happened when you cut in on one of the servicemen. Things happened so quick it was like someone had set off a fire alarm. Three of us always stuck together but we had our honour, your mates would stand back until three or four soldiers started in from all sides, then with a smile they would be there. I think in those days everybody took it as part of growing up, no one ever seemed to get hurt, but then no one used a knife or anything like that.

From Boscombe Down some of us were transferred to Upavon. It was a training place. Our job was to build a lot of new dog kennels. I was enjoying the job, they had a good canteen and the sun was shining, then one day I entered the canteen and there was a face I recognised.

"I thought I might find you here," said the Commander. "Can we sit over there in the corner? It won't take a minute. How would you like to take a refresher course, while you are here, on unarmed combat? We've got a little job coming up and we might need you. I can arrange it here on the camp, this could do you a bit of good."

I gave him my usual reply, "Do I have a choice?"

Well, it was all done very casually. Next day at lunch time a captain, in uniform, turned up and said, "I believe you would like to have a look round our gym." So off we went. I thought I was fit, but after fifteen minutes I thought I was going to die. My instructor said, "I thought you were good, that you just needed a few workouts."

"So did I," I replied.

After a few days I was over fit, I could not sleep at night, it took two weeks for my body to recover. Things began to get a bit difficult with the lads, they started to pull my leg, saying things like "Wot's she look like?" Well, I let them go on thinking.

Two weeks later the Commander was back and, as always, came straight to the point. "Have you used a hand pistol lately? You had better meet me at one p.m. in the firing range. Your record shows you are a first-class marksman."

"It also says I won't use a gun, sir," I told him.

"It won't do you any harm to get a little practice in," said the Commander.

The job was going quite well, it was an exciting place to work, everyday someone or something was dropping out of the sky on a parachute. We were there when one man's chute did not open and the next day a Land Rover came down quicker than it was expected. Then there was the training of the dogs, six hours every day.

We had just about finished the job and were loading all the surplus timber and tools on the lorry when I received a message saying, 'get a stomach ache or something, and report to the gym'. So off I go. When I arrived there were six people there, three of them I had never met.

The Commander took charge. "This is the plan – to go to Cornwall on Saturday night. A boat will arrive to pick up a load of arms. When loaded, it will be intercepted by two gunboats. The problem is, one of our men is on board and we have to get him off before the boat is boarded. So if you look at this model, we will go through the plan. We have a small rubber dinghy with two divers in that will follow the boat until the gun boats intercept it."

Then he turned to me and said, "Now, this is where you come in. Your job is to put out the searchlight on the gunboat on the right. By then, the dinghy will be up on the right-hand side of the boat. Our man on board will jump into the water and our two divers will fish him out and take him down the shoreline. Then we can all go home and leave the rest to the gunboats. Are there any questions?"

"How do we get there? What do I tell the wife, and how long will we be away?" I asked.

"Well, if all goes to plan you could be back home by Sunday lunch time. Tell your wife you've got to work on a job that can only be done at night. We will cover you if anything happens, and just come to work as usual," were his answers.

On Saturday morning I arrived at the gym to pick up the guns. I was given the rifle which I had been practising with during the week.

The Commander asked "What about your pistol?"

"I said I would practise with it, but not use it," I insisted.

We had a pleasant drive down to Cornwall and it was quite light when we arrived, which gave us time to look at the area in daylight. It looked just like a big cave to me, with not many people about.

"We have had confirmation that two lorries are on their way with the goods," said the Commander. "Well, I wish you luck. I will see you tomorrow." He put the pistol in my hand, "Just in case there is any trouble," and was gone. I didn't think he would stay – he never had before.

We had about three hours to wait and I started to think about where we were. I thought I knew this place. I think it's a place near Portwrinkle. It was getting dark when the news came through that the lorries had arrived. Looking out to sea we saw a light moving towards us. There was a wooden platform with iron rails with some sort of track leading to it across the sand. I'll say this for them, they were good at what they were doing, the boat was in, the lorries were unloaded and gone and in all it took them about twenty minutes. Then the boat made out to sea and from nowhere two gun boats appeared and on came the search lights. As I took aim, machine guns opened up from both sides of the boat. Out went the search lights on both the gunboats. It must have caused quite a panic on board those gunboats. By the time they got over the shock, most of the people on board had jumped into the sea and were swimming for shore.

Myself, I just picked up my gear and made for the pick-up spot. As I was running along the beach there was a big bang. I learned later when the other lads got back it had all gone wrong, someone on board set the engines at full speed as the rest of the crew had jumped into the sea. The two gun boats took off after the boat, leaving time for most of the crew to get back to shore. Some were picked up, but one chap managed to hide with the Captain until the onshore gang thought they had picked up any one still alive. So it turned out a waste of time for us, but the Commander did not think so, as we had done our job, or they had done it for us, as he said, "We got our chap out and no one knows who he is, and we never fired a shot!"

Glyn went on to build houses for Henfords in Shaftesbury in the 70s. When the housing market went flat, he left this job as there was not enough work to keep him busy.

There was a period of unemployment when he may have written the story.

He then went on to take a 1/4 share of a business – Scanmaster – Beanacre Car Spares – which he part-owned and managed.

His knees became increasingly painful and he was advised that if he could retire, to do so and enjoy himself for a few years. In 1990 he did so. In 2007 he was diagnosed with Parkinson's, back-dated eight years. He died on Jan 8th 2015.

He never told his family, and this story remained unknown until his wife discovered it late 2017 and read it for the first time.

The Author